What's the buzz?

"*50 Ways to Leave Your Mother* is a perfect little volume that delivers tons of essential advice and smart tips about everyone's ultimate rite of passage... a hoot to read, yet stays on message all the way... wish I'd had this book when I left... my transition would have been a lot smoother!"

–Tom McNulty, author of *Clean Like A Man*

"Tuck this wise, warm book in your grown kid's back pocket - it will provide a little extra padding and a lot of laughter in case the door hits them on the way out of your house!"

–Jane Adams, Ph.D.,
author of *When Our Grown Kids Disappoint Us: Letting Go Of Their Problems, Loving Them Anyway, and Getting On With Our Lives*

Published by Mother Love Publishing Company

1st printing, 2006. 2nd printing, 2007

Library of Congress Catalog Number 2006923966

ISBN: 0-9778178-9-X
ISBN: 978-0-9778178-9-4

Buy books at:
www.fiftywaysbooks.com

50 Ways to Leave your Mother

by Chris Salditt

illustrated by **Mike Force**

"I take the practical view of raising children. I put a sign in each of their rooms: Check-out time is 18 years."

- Erma Bombeck

This book is dedicated to Gene
and Angie LeTendre. Thanks
Mom and Dad for a lifetime of
unconditional love and support.

mother love publishing

Mukilteo, Washington

Acknowledgments

First and foremost, I'd like to thank my daughters, Katie Wall and Annie Salditt, whose life experiences—both good and bad—prompted me to write this book. For his encouragement and support, marketing advice, and technical skills, many thanks to my husband Phil. Thank you to Kris Jones for encouraging and motivating me to continue with this project when my confidence was in a slump, and for being a taskmaster extraordinaire when needed. To my friends and family: Mary Jo Froehlig, Elizabeth Koenig, Jeanne Rupel, Carrie Schroeder, Shannon Jay, Kathleen LeTendre, Janet Mills, Mary Beth Moze, and Pam Palasz—many thanks for your valued opinions and proofreading skills, and your patience with me no matter how many times I requested them. To Toni Baumann, Cara Biden, Mike and Kitty Harwick, the best friends anyone could have, sincere thanks for your vote of confidence and support. For legal advice and encouragement, thank you to Elizabeth Berns, attorney at law. And last, a big thank-you to Mike Force, not only for his artistic talents, but also for the enthusiasm and dedication he brought to this project.

Did you know?

- Roommates use your stuff, forget to pay the cable bill, and leave the front door unlocked most of the time. Oh yeah, and they don't buy toilet paper when it's their turn either.

- Landlords charge a penalty if the rent is late, don't always fix things when they break, and expect you to leave the place in better condition than when you moved in.

- Tomatoes cost $3 a pound, potatoes explode in the oven if not poked before baking, and it's a bad idea to grocery shop when you're hungry.

Read on for ways to deal with these problems and many more situations that might pop up on the journey from your parents' home to a life on your own.

Table of Contents

KEEP OUT

CHAPTER 1

So, It's Time to Move Out

You got a suitcase as a subtle hint from your parents, you don't like checking in with them when you're out past midnight, and you're embarrassed to tell your dates that you still live at home. Maybe it's time to make a move, but where do you start? Read on for tips on preparing for a move, what you'll need for starters, and how to get it all together.

1.

Your little sister is driving you crazy, and Grandma expects you to watch "Wheel of Fortune" with her every night. You've got to get out of there, but can you really afford to move out? Make a list of your expenses like car upkeep, student loan, and cell phone. Ask Mom and Dad for advice since they've been paying the bills for decades and can give reliable estimates for food and utility costs. (If you are not an experienced food shopper, you have no idea how expensive it is to feed you.) They'll also fill you in on all the miscellaneous expenses you might not think of, like haircuts, laundry, and medicine for your next cold.

HOUSEHOLD ITEMS

Light Bulbs	Broom
Batteries	Vacuum Cleaner
Fire Extinguisher	Paper Towels
Plunger	Laundry Soap
Toilet Brush	Dish Soap
Mop & Bucket	Cleaning Wipes

2.

Okay, you're going ahead with the move. Start collecting toiletries, nonperishable foods, and household products. Money will be tight when you begin paying rent. Stocking up on supplies now will ease the money crunch a bit so you might not have to wash both your hair and your clothes with the same soap.

Tip

Check internet sites and newspaper classifieds for typical rents in your area. If you survive this reality check and still think you are able to move out, read on.

Tip

Be thorough. For example, car expenses include: car payment, insurance, gas, oil changes, parking, and repairs. Is a bus pass starting to sound good yet?

Tip

Be honest with yourself. If there is something you are unwilling to live without, like your daily designer coffee drink or cell phone, add that expense to your list.   Factor in the costs that will be split with room-mates, like cable, rent and toilet paper.

3.

Encourage your parents to buy in bulk. Surely they won't begrudge you a few rolls of toilet paper when they've just bought the forty-eight-roll pack. The same goes for the thirty-pack of microwave popcorn and the twelve-pack of canned tuna. You get the idea.

4.

Let relatives, family friends, and neighbors know that you're moving out and you'd be happy to take their unwanted household items and furniture. Point out they'll be cleaning out their garages and basements at the same time.

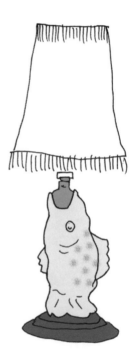

Tip

Start a new tradition. Have family members throw a "moving out" shower. The result: cool stuff for your new place.

KITCHEN ITEMS

Metal & Rubber Spatulas	Measuring Spoons
Mixing Spoons	Bottle Opener
Cookie Sheet	Corkscrew
Cooking Pots	Can Opener
Fry Pan	Pot Holders
Electric Hand Mixer	Dishes
Potato Peeler	Glasses
Sharp Knives	Coffee Maker
Cutting Board	Espresso Machine
Baking Pans (8x8 & 9x13)	Basic Cookbook
Strainer/Colander	Measuring Cups

5.

*C**heck** curbside, especially in college neighborhoods, for castoffs to furnish your apartment. You might just find that mustard-yellow velour recliner—a college staple—that will go perfectly with the plush, avocado-green sofa from Aunt Agnes.*

BINGO!

Tip

A little bug spray, a spritz of upholstery deodorizer, an old blanket, or some duct tape will remedy most furniture flaws.

6.

Your parents' lifestyle has afforded you many everyday conveniences that you'll have to provide for yourself or do without. So, get that toilet plunger before you actually need it. The alternative solution to that problem is not pretty. All the stuff that was just there all those years—scissors and tape, bandages and aspirin, can opener and batteries—will not magically appear at your new place. This is where parents who buy in bulk can help out, or they might have a spare flashlight or hammer that you can have.

TOOL KIT

Hammer
Screwdrivers (Phillips & regular)
Pliers
Nails & Screws (variety pack)
Picture Hangers
Blu-tac (for hanging posters)
Flashlight with Batteries
Masking Tape
Duct Tape
Super Glue
Tape Measure (metal)

7.

Are you getting the idea that moving out is going to be more expensive than you thought? Put away cash to pay some of your initial costs—rent deposits, moving costs, and first month's bills—while you might still actually have some extra money. It may be many years before you live this well again. It all seems like a big sacrifice, but it'll all be worth it.

FIRST AID

Bandages
Antibacterial Cream
Digital Thermometer
Pain Relievers
Aloe Vera Cream
Heating Pad or Rice Pack

Vaporizer (cool mist)
Tweezers
Cold Pack (Frozen veggies
   work well too.)
Basic First Aid Book

8.

Box up childhood treasures that won't fit in the 8'x10' bedroom you most likely will inhabit. Ask your parents (nicely) to store your Little League trophies and rock collection just until you get a bigger place in a year or two. (It'll be more like a decade or two, but unless they have older kids who've already pulled this, they'll probably believe you.)

9.

Get a couple of lessons from Mom or Dad on using the washer and dryer, as well as sorting and folding (Hah!) clothes. Take time to read the labels for water temperature and drying instructions to prevent laundry disasters like turning your entire wardrobe pink or shrinking clothes three sizes. When in doubt, use cold water to wash clothes; stains won't set and clothes won't shrink.

SEWING KIT

Needles

Thread (assorted colors)

Scissors

Safety and Straight Pins

Iron-on Mending Tape

Tape Measure

Pin Cushion

10.

If you don't have a checking account, get one. Enter all transactions in your check register, including bank charges, and get overdraft protection. If all else fails, throw your bank statements in a shoe box, along with all cash withdrawal and deposit receipts. Then you'll know where to find them if you ever need them (but hope you don't).

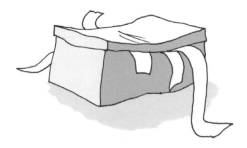

Tip

Check your credit rating online. Identity theft is here to stay and checking your credit every year eliminates surprises and headaches in the long run. Free credit reports are available.
Try www.annualcreditreport.com.

11.

A reliable alarm clock is a must. Get a second one as a back up. Ideally one should be electric and the other battery-operated. That way, if the power goes out or the battery dies, you still have one working clock. It's not a bad idea to set alarms on cell phones and watches, too. It may seem like overkill, but Mommy and Daddy won't be there to wake you up. You can't afford to be late for work or classes now that you're paying the bills.

Tip

Get a calendar to remind you what day it is, when rent is due, and when it's Mom's or Dad's birthday.

CHAPTER 2

Looking for a Place of Your Own—
Real World or Animal House?

You told your parents you're moving out, and they've put the "room for rent" sign in the front yard. There's no turning back now. This chapter will give you suggestions for finding the right neighborhood, protecting your rights as a renter, and deciding whether to bring your pet, CoCo, or just leave him tied to your closet door back home for your parents to deal with.

12.

Since you probably won't be living in conditions remotely comparable to your parents' home, downsize your housing expectations to what you can realistically afford. If your budget screamed *'85 Buick Skylark*, would you punish yourself by looking at a new *Porsche*?

Tip

If you absolutely cannot find anything
to rent in your price range, consider
taking on another roommate to share
expenses, but be wary of cramming
your place with too many people.
Can you say "Animal House?"

13.

Unless you're moving to an established household (friends, co-workers or strangers who took pity on you), you'll have to investigate potential neighborhoods. Get out of the car and walk around, day and night, to get a feel for safety, conveniences, and the "hip" factor (if that sort of thing is important to you). Are there lots of people around your age or does it feel like a retirement community?

SIGNS THAT YOU'RE LOOKING IN THE <u>WRONG</u> NEIGHBORHOOD

- There's a Walgreens on every other corner.
- Walkers are parked in the bike racks.
- Large print editions are featured prominently in the bookstore window.
- The hair salon is named "Flo's" or "Curl Up and Dye."
- You notice there is an abundance of handicap parking spaces, all filled with *Cadillacs*, *Lincolns*, and minivans.
- The lawns are extremely well-manicured and decorated with wishing wells, gnomes and plastic flowers.
- Every restaurant advertises Early Bird Specials.
- The ads in the supermarket windows are for dried plums, bran cereals and adult diapers.
- The streets are deserted after 6 o'clock in the evening.

Tip

Check bulletin boards in restaurants, grocery stores, and coffee shops in the neighborhoods you like for rental and roommate-wanted ads.

Tip

Signs outside rental properties usually include the manager's phone number and vacancy information. Call for details on decent ones— like those with four walls and a roof.

There's an old saying:

"If it sounds too good to be true, it probably is." Guess what? This also applies to rental ads. Be a bit skeptical about just what an ad promises.

What it says:	*What it really means:*
Cozy	It's so small you might mistake it for a closet.
Clean	Is that the best thing they can say about it?
Centrally Located	It's above the teriyaki joint in the *middle* of the strip mall.
Great View	It has a window.
Spacious	You can fit the bed in the room and still open the door.
Charming	It hasn't been remodeled since 1950.
Newly Remodeled	It has a new shower curtain and toilet seat.

14.

Keep track of all places you've called, cross off the real losers, and list the details of any promising ones. You'll want to know how much the rent is, what's included in the price, number of rooms/bedrooms, occupancy date, deposit amounts and other charges like credit check, pets, parking and smoking, if applicable. Did they use any of the no-no words, like charming, cozy, or clean?

Tip

If you are a smoker, don't forget to include the cost of cigarettes or nicotine patches in your monthly budget. Talk about an eye opener!

Tip

Hidden costs to consider:

- Laundry facilities? Are they in-unit or somewhere on the premises? (Hopefully they're not in a dark and scary basement.) Free? If not, how much?
- Parking space or garage available? Free? If not, how much? (Hope there's enough parking for everyone so you don't have to beat them home every night for a spot.)
- Utilities (heat, electricity, water, trash) included? If not, average monthly cost?

Tip

If the heat bill is high, make a pact with room-mates to keep heat on low and wear jackets or sweaters in cold months—really.

Tip

To save on laundry expenses, wash clothes at your parents' home when you make your weekly raid on their refrigerator.

15.

***I**ntent* to vacate rules vary from state to state. Know the law and then pick the right time of month to call landlords. If twenty days is the rule, then call around the 10th of the month to get the "pick of the litter" in rentals. Some states require thirty or even sixty days notice; call those places between the first and fifth of the month for best results.

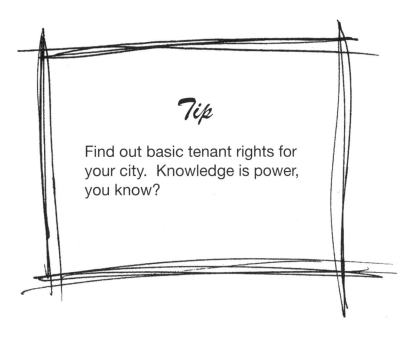

Tip

Find out basic tenant rights for your city. Knowledge is power, you know?

16.

Give yourself enough time to find a decent place, or you'll end up with the "leftovers" — the places that are dumps, in bad neighborhoods or way too expensive. There's a reason why they're still available this late in the month.

Tip

If you've zeroed in on a hot property, visit the building at various times to check it out. It's possible some nut lives next door, it's very noisy (kids crying, people fighting, polkas playing), or parking is impossible to find. It could be that none of these things were going on when you looked at the place during the day when adults were working, children were in school, and the polka classics hour was not on the radio.

17.

Jf the current tenants are home while you're looking at the place, ask their opinion on the landlord or manager. If you know in advance that he's uncooperative, slow to fix problems, or a snoop, you might want to pass on that place. No one needs the landlord from hell if they can avoid it.

18.

You think you've found the perfect place. Add the cost of your share of the rent and utilities, parking, and laundry to your existing list of monthly obligations. (You remember, the one suggested at the beginning of this book?) When added to your estimates for food, car maintenance, and other "must haves" like cell phone and internet connection, can you still afford to move out? You've come too far to quit now! Besides, your parents already have plans for your room.

Tip

You may be asked to pay for a credit check—to make sure you aren't a deadbeat—when you fill out a rent application. This amount will not be refunded even if you do not get the apartment. Who said life was fair?

Tip

Be prepared for a negative reaction from your parents when they see the place you've chosen. "Where did we go wrong?" or "How can I possibly sleep at night while you are living in that place?" may be uttered. They've forgotten what their first place looked like. Hey, this *is* their first place!

19.

Time to sign on the dotted line. Be prepared to come up with a huge chunk of change. It varies, but you may be asked for first and last month's rent, damage and cleaning deposits, and pet deposit (if little CoCo is coming along).

Tip

Disclose any pets you plan to bring to live in the apartment. It won't be easy to disguise your pet Komodo Dragon (CoCo?) as a foot stool.

Tip

Get everything in writing and receipts for all money you lay out. Find out where and when to pay the rent, when a late fee penalty goes into effect and how much it is. (It could be sizable, possibly $100 or more.) Remember, beer and latte money is at stake.

Tip

Keep your valuable papers – lease agreement, tax returns, and prom pictures – in a safe place. Those small metal boxes sold at office supply stores work well and are fireproof. If you are really disorganized, give copies to Mom or Dad for safekeeping.

STATIONERY SUPPLIES

Pens and Pencils

Note Pads

Stapler and Staples

Scissors

Tape

Push Pins

Paper Clips

Bulletin Board

Glue

Metal Document Box

Calendar

Envelopes

Stamps

Tip

Want to avoid most of the hassles of finding a place, picking roommates and laying out money for deposits? Find a friend, or friend of a friend, or the name of a stranger off the coffee shop bulletin board who needs an additional roommate and avoid all or most of these deposits. This situation works best for someone low on funds or furniture but desperate to leave home.

20.

You've been given the keys to your new place. Cover your butt! Insist on a walk-through to check for existing damages. Bring a parent or friend along to catch what you might miss. It's important to fill out a detailed damage report and return it promptly to management. Include every stain on the carpet, crack in a mirror, and scratch on the woodwork, or risk being charged for it when you move out. Both you and the manager or landlord should keep a signed and dated copy. Then put yours in the metal box along with your lease agreement.

Tip

Take photos of any damage—with the date feature on your camera in place—and keep as proof of existing damage. Just whip them out when, on the day you move out, your landlord tries to deduct that broken window from your damage deposit. Gotcha!

Tip

It's possible the landlord might offer to take care of damages or promise to reimburse you for fixing them. The best time to get their attention—and satisfactory results—is *before* you move in. Be persistent. Once you've moved in he won't try as hard to please you, and that bathroom toilet might leak until the day you move out—and then he'll try to make you pay for breaking it!

CHAPTER 3

Roommates—The Good, the Bad, and the Tolerable

You've found a place to live, but there's no way you can afford it without a couple of roommates. There's a lot to discuss with prospective roommates, like do you share food, who gets the big bedroom, and how many nights in a row can their friends crash on the couch before you get really ticked off? Will the new roommates let you put up your string of chili pepper lights in the kitchen? It doesn't hurt to ask, and this chapter has a lot of answers, just not that one.

21.

You're moving away from your parents' home and, to lessen your financial burden, you're getting one or more roommates. What do you know about the people you'll be living with? Are they party people or loners, slobs or neat freaks, classical or heavy metal? Investigate before committing. What are you willing to put up with?

Tip

A lie detector test for prospective roommates would solve a lot of problems. Unfortunately, they are still too expensive for all but law enforcement (and reality TV) purposes at this time. You'll just have to trust your gut for now.

A GOOD ROOMMATE...

- Has cute, available siblings or friends with dating potential.
- Is a master chef.
- Has a car.
- Cleans for a hobby.
- Has a compulsion to please.
- Has a trust fund.
- Has cool furniture.
- Shares your taste in music.
- Has state of the art electronics.
- Wears your size clothing and has a great wardrobe.
- Has famous friends.
- Is not quite as cute as you.

A BAD ROOMMATE...

- Has personal hygiene problems.
- Doesn't work or go to school and would be home all the time.
- Thinks he's cool or funny when he's not.
- Loves to cook organ meats like liver, cow tongue and sheep stomach on a regular basis. Hey, it could happen!
- Is too popular and would bring dates and large crowds of friends over constantly.
- Uses irritating slang words in every sentence, uh, like he's hella ghetto, ya know?
- Eats things that are not food, like toenails, dryer lint and wax.
- Is a practicing nudist but doesn't have a good body.
- Listens to music you cannot tolerate. (Is Vanilla Ice still recording?)
- Sleeps all day and parties all night. You'll get tired of stepping over the pizza boxes every morning.

22.

U*tilize* multiple sources for finding potential roommates:

- School friend
- Co-worker
- Relative
- Internet-based networks (myspace, craigslist)
- Acquaintance from the gym, church or dance class
- Bulletin boards at school, coffee shop,
  post office (uh-oh)

Why best friends don't always make ideal roommates:

- They think your invitations are their invitations too.
- They assume your friends are actually phoning to talk to them, not you.
- You may never be alone again, and constantly sneaking out of the house to avoid them is no fun.
- They may have a friendly relationship with your parents or love interest and could accidentally spill some of your secrets to them.
- It's hard to impress your new friends with stories of your reign as prom queen and class president in high school when your best friend is with you constantly and she knows that you were a loser in school.

23.

Invent sample questions for prospective roommates:

? If a train is traveling at forty miles per hour, with winds from the north at twenty miles per hour, and I've left my personal journal on the coffee table, do you read it?

? Do you listen to opera, Celtic, or polkas? If so, would you consider wearing headphones when listening to your music?

? If my significant other flirts with you when I leave the room, do you:

(a.) Run screaming from the room?

(b.) Slip him your private phone number?

(c.) Make a date and send me instead?

? My mother stops by with a plate of cookies. Do you:

(a.) Put them in my room and not give them a second thought?

(b.) Eat a couple, then rearrange the remainder of the cookies to fill in the gap?

(c.) Eat them all, throw away the plate, and deny ever seeing the cookies?

24.

Honesty is the best policy with potential roommates. Reveal any quirky habits you have, like meditating in the nude at 6 a.m.—complete with incense and chanting—or that you are a chronic whistler . . . of Broadway show tunes.

Topics for discussion between roommates:

- Message-taking (Lives have been lost over this!)
- Shared expenses and bill-paying (Hint—pick the most responsible person.)
- Noise levels (Huh? Did you say something?)
- Sleepovers (Who's that guy on the couch?!)
- Parties (Polka, cocktail or *Tupperware*? It makes a big difference.)
- Food (Sharing/not sharing, and consequences, as in "Who's the jerk that ate my last frozen waffle?")
- Alcohol (This is very important if you're twenty-one and any other roommates are younger.)
- Smoking (It might be hard to get additional roommates if you do smoke.)
- Morning Person or Night Owl (A perky early-riser doesn't mix well with an insomniac.)
- Clean or Messy (Will it be necessary to wear flip flops in the shower?)
- Punk or Pop (Hint: Do they have a spiked Mohawk or a ponytail with a scrunchie?)
- Pets (Goldfish sure. Monkey, not so good.)

Tip

Even if your new roommate swears he doesn't have a pet, you might want to investigate if you:

- Start sneezing every time you walk past his room.
- Go searching for the container of granola and find *Tender Vittles* instead.
- Hear baby talk or kissing sounds coming from his room when he is alone and not on the phone.
- Notice he goes out for short walks at all hours of the day and night, and always wears a bulky jacket when he does so.
- Routinely experience a not-so-fresh smell wafting from his room.

Let's face it. If he does any of these things, and doesn't have a pet, you've still got a serious roommate problem to deal with.

Tip

Talk over stuff that bugs you right away. Don't wait until you can't stand the sight of each other to blow up over a botched phone message. Big deal, so "Mr. Right" never calls again.

Tip

Agree on a plan for overnight guests. Is once in awhile okay? Or is it time to start charging Joe's girlfriend rent?

25.

Respect each other's space. If he says not to use his razor, don't. Remember how your dad always knew when you used his?

Tip

If you don't want them eating your favorite ice cream, mark the container "tofu" and chances are they will leave it alone.

26.

Don't depend on your roommate to restock the toilet tissue when it's his turn. Keep a secret stash in your room for emergency use. When all else fails, borrow a roll from your parents or your favorite bar or restaurant. (But that would be wrong.)

Tip

Don't try "borrowing" one of those humongous rolls of toilet paper used in many public restrooms. They're impossible to conceal under today's tight-fitting fashions.

Tip

No two roommates should have the same color toothbrush. And, if yours is wet when you haven't used it recently: (a) run very hot water over it for thirty seconds; (b) cycle it through the dishwasher; or (c) throw it away and get a new one. Maybe you need to keep it in your room, right next to the expensive shampoo you're not sharing with your roommates.

27.

Replace or return borrowed items to your roommates ASAP, and in their original condition. But if you can't do so, think up a good excuse, like:

(a.) You were abducted by aliens while wearing her sweater, and they kept it for research purposes.

(b.) The refrigerator stopped working and you were forced to eat everything in it to prevent spoilage.

(c.) You had to flush her favorite pair of false eyelashes when the cat accidentally knocked them in the toilet.

28.

Assign each roommate a shelf in the fridge and cupboard. All other food is off limits. If you absolutely have to eat your roommate's last fudge pop, please replace it as soon as possible…and maybe leave a note.

29.

Include all interested roommates in decorating the place. It will feel more like home to everyone. Many people will draw the line at the "dorm room" look or plastic covering on the sofa, so don't get your hopes up.

THRIFT STORE CHIC

30.

Establish ownership of household items early on. It's easy to forget who brought what, and you do want to hang on to Aunt Shirley's hand-crocheted doilies forever.

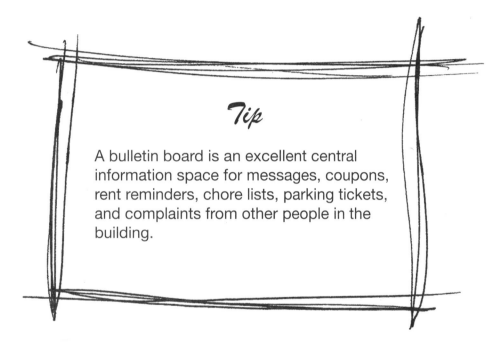

Tip

A bulletin board is an excellent central information space for messages, coupons, rent reminders, chore lists, parking tickets, and complaints from other people in the building.

31.

Don't give your door key to just anyone. Roommates should know who has keys to their place. And keep the doors locked – it's a jungle out there!

32.

Seldom are all the bedrooms in a home the same size. Reach an understanding before you move in as to who gets the best room. Be prepared to pay more for the bigger room or the better view. Another option is to trade off halfway through the year. The problem is, that when the time comes to trade, even the person who now gets the better room thinks it's too much work. You must do the trade, and it is so worth it.

Tip

There should be an established
location for all mail that comes
in. No one wants to find their tax
refund check behind the sofa six
months later. The same goes for
birthday checks from your parents.

CHAPTER 4

Smooth Move

*L*earn how to make moving day—a huge inconvenience for just about everyone—as painless as possible. Find out how to keep your movers happy and where to pack your "blankie" so you'll have it to sleep with that first night in your new place. There's even information on what kind of shower curtain not to buy.

33.

O*nce* you know your move-in date, get your friends with trucks and vans—and anyone under seventy-five—to commit before they can think up a good excuse for not helping you.

34.

If you will need a moving truck, reserve one immediately. They go quickly at the end of the month, and you don't want to drive to the next state to pick one up. You can always cancel if you are lucky enough to start dating someone with a truck or van.

Tip

Helping friends move is right up there with driving friends to the airport, so treat your helpers well. Feed them, supply plenty of cold drinks, and let them choose the music.

35.

Don't put off packing until the last minute. Boxes from the grocery store work well. Mark each box with contents and the room it belongs in at the new place. Your moving buddies will appreciate that, and they may even help you move again… and you *will* move again.

Tip

Be prepared to help these same friends move when it's their turn. Hey, it's only fair.

36.

Pack one box with stuff you'll need for your first night in your new place, like bedding, towels, soap, and your teddy bear. You'll be getting off to a bad start if you use your roommate's toothbrush the very first night you live there.

Tip

Don't forget to buy a shower curtain.
And don't alienate your roommates by
getting one that is see-through.

37.

*G*et change of address forms at the Post Office and send them out at least four weeks in advance. This goes for driver's license, voter registration, bank accounts and credit cards, and anyone else that regularly sends you mail. Give your new address to your relatives too, so they will know where to send your birthday checks.

38.

Buy an address book and add info for all friends and family. It's important for you to send thank-you notes for those birthday checks.

39.

Be prepared to clean your new place before you move in. The last people left it dirty, and although they didn't get their damage deposit back, you can bet the manager didn't get it cleaned either. Besides, everyone's idea of clean is different, and you'll want to start out with just your own germs.

MAKE FRIENDS WITH THE MICROWAVE – FAST

CHAPTER 5

The Care and Feeding of Your Face— or "Reality Bites"

For many of you leaving home for the first time, getting fed will be the biggest challenge. Food will no longer magically appear in the fridge or on the table each day. It's up to you to figure out what you want to eat, what you can afford to eat, and how much you're willing to do to prepare it. This chapter will give you help with all your food dilemmas, and even tell you how to bake a potato, a very good thing to know.

40.

*T**he** best foods are expensive. Bread, noodles, and rice are cheap, while tomatoes, steak, and Cocoa Puffs are luxuries. Eat those foods when others feed you in their homes, at restaurants, and at cousin Leroy's wedding.

Tip

Say yes to leftovers and doggie bags.

41.

Carrots, apples, and potatoes are good food investments. They are relatively cheap, healthy, and good-tasting, and will last for weeks in the fridge, long after your food money for the month has run out and the milk has gone bad.

PANTRY ITEMS

Cooking Oil	Basic Spices
Cereal	Sugar
Popcorn Seeds	Flour
Microwave Popcorn	Cans of:
Ramen Noodles	Soup
Peanut Butter	Tuna
Rice	Beans
Macaroni and Cheese	Tomatoes (diced)
Pasta Noodles	Broth

42.

U*nless* you are conducting a science experiment, black, green, and "fuzzy" foods in the fridge need to be tossed out. That goes for plastic bags of liquid-like mystery substances and containers that bulge and fizz or gurgle when opened, or . . . oh, never mind!

Tip

Two lifesavers are ramen noodles and microwave popcorn because they are cheap, filling, and ready in minutes.

43.

The freezer is your friend. Inexpensive frozen veggies satisfy Mom's demands that you eat your vegetables, and you can take out just what you need each time. It's a good way to store bread too.

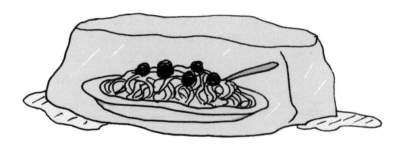

"DEFROSTING LEFTOVERS"

Tip

A coffee maker is a great investment. Lattes and Mochas, while delicious, can really set you back.

($3/day per cup x 365 days = $1,095/year plus tip)

If you're feeling deprived, ask for an espresso machine for your birthday and make your own designer drinks at home. Don't cry. You can still go out for coffee, just not so often.

44.

To save money, eat out less. Learn to boil water, and then advance to tea, pudding, toast and boiled eggs. Graduate to more complicated dishes like baked potatoes, oatmeal, and pancakes.

HOW TO MAKE A BAKED POTATO

- Wash outside skin of one or more medium baking potatoes. (Russets are good.)
- Prick each potato with a fork 3-4 times.
- Place on rack in an oven preheated to 400 degrees and bake for one hour.
- To test, poke with fork. If it slides in easily, the potato is done.

45.

Shop for groceries from a list, and don't stray from it unless you have:

(a.) Just won the lottery.
(b.) A car to transport all those bags of food.
(c.) Your mom along and she's paying for all your groceries.

TRUE OR FALSE?

(Answers follow but don't peek.)

(1.) It's best to shop when hungry because it will be easier to remember all the favorite snack foods you've been craving.

(2.) If you're in a hurry to eat, crank your oven up an extra 200 degrees so the food cooks faster. This works especially well with frozen foods.

(3.) Ramen noodles are nature's perfect food. As a bonus, the high sodium content helps you retain fluids so you won't get dehydrated.

(4.) Toasting moldy bread will burn off the mold, making it okay to eat. Besides, mold has needed vitamins and minerals and adds texture to food.

(5.) It's okay to put metal containers in the microwave. Warnings against this are just urban myths promoted by the makers of plastic wrap and glass cookware.

(They are all false.)

CHAPTER 6

Wheels of (Mis)Fortune

The decision to take your car with you will be a no-brainer if you move to a rural area or one that doesn't have public transportation. This chapter presents several scenarios where having a car is one big pain in the butt, so if you have access to buses, light rail or a bicycle, you might want to think twice about owning a car. But since you most likely will have to learn the hard way, read on for ways to avoid some auto pitfalls by using a little common sense.

46.

In your situation—city, country, or suburbs—is it wise to have a car, or would public transportation serve you better? Waiting in ferry lines, paying for or finding parking, and car maintenance costs all should be considered before taking a car to your new home. If money is no object, or your "soul mate" will drop you for not having a car, then by all means, keep your car!

Tip

Pick a roommate who has a car and stay on his good side. Maybe he'll take you places once in awhile. Those twelve-packs of drinks get pretty heavy after walking a mile, and your pizza will be stone cold by the time you get it home by bus.

47.

Get an emergency road service membership. You most likely have a "vintage" car with a good chance of breaking down on a regular basis. They will come to your rescue if you run out of gas, leave your lights on, or lock your keys in the car, all very possible scenarios for the poor and the partiers (your people).

Tip

Remember, if you live in an area that experiences snow and cold in the winter, it's very possible that your new place will not have a garage or even a covered parking area. That means shoveling your car out of snowbanks, scraping ice from windshields, and spending money on antifreeze, windshield cleaner and stuff to keep your gas line from freezing.

48.

Pay attention to where you park your car. Getting it towed is a mind-numbing experience. That sinking feeling when you realize your car is gone, and probably not stolen—remember you have a "vintage" car—is awful. Fines and towing charges will cancel out your latte or movie money for months to come, plus it's a real hassle to get your car back.

Tip

Did you know the impound lot where your car was towed will continue to charge you a daily storage fee until you pick up the car? That's in addition to the fine for parking illegally and the tow charge. So get that car back as soon as possible.

Tip

Know how to check your oil and get regular oil changes. Pay attention to those warning lights on the dash. By now your "vintage" car may be burning oil, and running out of oil is a very bad thing.

49.

Get a bus schedule for routes from home to work and school. You can't afford to miss work—you have financial responsibilities now—if your car isn't working or you can't remember where you parked it. Your parents' garage was so much easier to find.

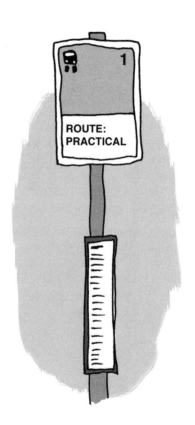

ROUTE:
PRACTICAL

Tip

Keep car insurance and registration current. Proof of both should be kept in your car's glove box, right next to those little ketchup and mustard packets you've been saving.

Tip

Put "Mom" type bumper stickers on your car. "My child is an honor student" is a good one. This just might protect you in parking and other ticketing situations. Hey, it couldn't hurt.

50.

Keep emergency road supplies, jumper cables, jack, and spare tire in your trunk. Mom and Dad might not live close by—or feel inclined to help you at 4 a.m.—like they might have when you lived at home. Life was so much simpler then, wasn't it?

"LAUNDRY DAY"

CHAPTER 7

Tricks, Manipulations,
and Other Short Cuts

There's very valuable info here on how to elicit sympathy from those who love you, get free stuff, and generally come out ahead. There's something for everybody in this chapter. Anyone who uses all ten tips is a real master manipulator, but you wouldn't want to buy a used car from him or have him marry your sister.

1.

You want to wear your favorite shirt for a big date tonight but it's dirty. Solution: wear it when you take your shower. Scrub as you would your skin. Lather, rinse and repeat. Don't try this with "cold water wash" clothing; the shock will kill you!

Tip

Emergency Clothes-Drying Solutions:

- Hang wet clothing out the window, with a small piece of fabric pressed between window sill and closed window. Make sure all contact areas of the window are clean. Hope for a mildly breezy day.
- Use a hair dryer. This works best if the clothing is on a hanger or shower rod, rather than on your body. Yes, avoid burns and possible electrocution whenever possible.
- Take your shower early in the day and hang clothing to dry.
- Wear the clothing wet and hope no one notices. This works best in warm-weather months in dry climates.

2.

For quick clean-ups before your parents or current love interest come over, buy some of those disposable wipes available for dusting, disinfecting, glass-cleaning and more. If you are really rushed, simply spray some disinfectant in a few strategic places—kitchen, bathroom, your armpits—and they'll think you cleaned just for them. (Please don't really spray your armpits; it's just a joke.)

3.

W*ear* your underwear for three days. Turn inside out and wear three more days, then throw in trash. You must like inexpensive underwear or have no social life to speak of. For some reason, this tip appeals to guys more than girls.

4.

Wear wrinkled or dirty clothes to your parents' house. Your mother will be so mortified, and afraid the neighbors might see you, that she will wash and iron your clothes immediately. Try to wear several layers of clothing for bigger benefits. Don't do this too often though or she'll catch on.

5.

Flattery will get your everywhere. Compliment your host profusely for the meal and more invitations to dine will follow, as well as large packets of leftovers for you to take home. Examples:

(a.) "Nobody makes apple pie like you do, Grandma!"
(b.) "I've never seen such a beautiful beef roast in my life!"
(c.) "This is the best meal I have ever had!"
(d.) Oh boy, meat! I haven't had that in weeks!"
(This one will bring a tear to any mother's eye.)

6.

Never, ever brag to your relatives about how well you're doing. Pity reaps great rewards. Once they know you're doing well, you can say goodbye to free meals, gifts, and extra cash.

7.

*I*f you're really too busy or broke to do laundry, sneak a couple pieces of clothing into your roommate's laundry basket. She probably won't notice until she's folding the clothes. Practice looking innocent. Appropriate responses to her might be:

(a.) "Oh my, I've been looking all over for those."
(b.) "I must have left it behind in the washing machine."
(c.) "I didn't have my glasses on when I got undressed, and I must have accidentally put my clothes in your hamper."
Or, if she's really angry:
(d.) "Those aren't even my clothes. I have no idea where they came from."

8.

Accept invitations from Mom or Dad to go to the mall or grocery store. Chances are you will get something new to wear, a bag of groceries, a free lunch, or maybe all three.

9.

Find a job where you get free or discounted stuff that you couldn't otherwise afford. This frees up funds to spend on other things. Good employers are:

- Restaurants
- Movie theaters
- Supermarkets
- Hair Salons or Spas
- Doctor or Dentist Offices
- Car Repair Shops
- Laundromats
- Clothing and Department Stores
- Coffee Shops

10.

Remember to make a "wish list" for birthdays and other gift-giving occasions. Just make it appropriate for the giver's financial situation. The list should not be too long or you'll look greedy, a real turnoff to your family.

WISH LIST IDEAS

- Anything from the lists in this book
- Gift cards for groceries, music stores, discount stores, theaters, gas stations and coffee shops
- Basic cookbook
- Household hint/stain remover book
- Calendar with important dates entered
- Blankets, pillows, sheets
- Nostalgic gifts like your favorite childhood book or an album of family photos (very comforting when you're feeling homesick)
- Ski lift tickets or tickets to sporting events
- Music concert tickets
- Plane ticket to a favorite vacation destination or home if living far away
- Gift certificate for tattoo parlor (just kidding, sort of)

CHAPTER 8

Mom, We Just got Married by an Elvis Impersonator!

It won't take long for you to realize how good you had it when you lived with your parents. In most cases you still wouldn't go back home even if you had the chance, so you have little choice but to learn from your experiences and—yes, it must be said—grow up just a little bit. Use some of the ideas in this chapter to show off your newfound wisdom and pay back a little to people you have come to appreciate.

1.

If you plan to leave town or will be out of touch for more than a couple of days, let your parents or roommates know. That is unless you enjoy being the subject of a Missing Persons Report, or having your face plastered on a milk carton. Tell enough of the truth to prevent unnecessary panic from those who love you.

2.

Get a brief medical history from your parents if you will no longer be using their family doctor and dentist. Make a point to locate the nearest hospital, and ask friends for leads on a good doctor and dentist nearby. You might not have time to check the Yellow Pages for one if you have food poisoning or just injured yourself breakdancing.

3.

Save your spare change—a mayonnaise jar works nicely—and at the end of each month you should have a few bucks to spend. Depending on your financial situation—from "destitute" to "almost making it"—you can deposit the change in your savings account, splurge on a pizza, or replace all the food you've "borrowed" from your roommates.

← INSURANCE POLICY

Tip

There are numerous medical information sites on the internet that might help you to avoid a costly doctor visit in a non-emergency situation. Don't bother with this approach if you are bleeding profusely, in and out of consciousness, or otherwise in need of emergency care. In that case, get yourself to a hospital immediately.

4.

Take the advice in this book and actually write thank you notes for the dinners, birthday gifts, and pity checks you've received.

5.

C*all* your parents just to say hi and not to ask for any money, rides, or other favors.

6.

Jnvite your family to your house for dinner, even if it's just for a frozen pizza. Don't forget to bake it, and pass the napkins, paper towels, or toilet tissue for greasy fingers.

7.

Remember to send birthday cards to important people in your life. If you're too broke to buy cards, you can make them a collage from magazine clippings, or even just remember to call them on their special day.

8.

Wash and return plastic containers from leftovers to anyone who was nice enough to feed you. They'll be pleasantly surprised.

9.

*I*f you have a few bucks extra, for whatever reason:

(a.) Take Mom or Dad to breakfast or for coffee.
(b.) Buy the "budget bunch" of flowers—or even a single flower—at the supermarket for Mom or Grandma.
(c.) Bring dessert when invited for dinner. They'll be impressed even if it's from the day-old shelf.
(d.) Bake Mom or Dad a birthday cake. A box mix is fine and some brands even have a baking pan right in the box.

10.

Really freak out your parents when visiting them. Take the garbage out, empty the dishwasher, or offer to cut the grass. Be prepared to pick them up off the floor after they've fainted from the shock of it all.

"When I was a boy of fourteen, my father was so ignorant that I could hardly stand to have the old man around. But when I got to be twenty-one, I was astonished by how much the old man had learned in seven years."

—Josh Billings
aka Henry Wheeler Shaw
19th century humorist & lecturer

Copies of *50 Ways to Leave Your Mother* can be purchased at www.fiftywaysbooks.com

If you have an experience or tip to share about your move out on your own, the author would love to hear from you. Please send a brief summary of your experience, along with your contact information to:

Chris Salditt
c/o Mother Love Publishing
PO Box 1547
Mukilteo, WA 98275

or email: chris@fiftywaysbooks.com

Chris Salditt has successfully launched her own two daughters to independence, using their experiences to fill the pages of this book. She's given them advice on how to handle a greedy landlord, bake a potato to perfection, and understand the mysteries of the ramen noodle and popcorn diet. Chris lives with her husband in a Seattle suburb, just far enough away from her daughters to mind her own business, yet close enough to offer a "mommy fix" when needed.

www.fiftywaysbooks.com

Mike Force is an illustrator and designer from Seattle. He successfully moved out of his parent's house to Brooklyn where he illustrated and designed *Welcome to the Land of Cannibalistic Horses* (Puberty Press, 2004). He wishes he had read *50 Ways to Leave your Mother* many years ago.

www.mikeforce.org